A Holy Experiment

David Holdsworth

BookLeaf
Publishing

Presentation by *BookLeaf Publishing*

Web: www.bookleafpub.com

E-mail: info@bookleafpub.com

ISBN: 9789395755061

First edition 2022

DEDICATION

To my beloved wife Sarah:

Nature, gentle wild things and you.

The things that I love so true.

Walk with me through the woods of life.

Hand in hand we will take the strife.

Across the valley to the babbling brooks.

I will admire your kind looks.

Into the wild lands where nature is king.

Our love will make us sing.

My angelic beloved, you are beautiful forever.
Intertwined I will leave you never.

Nature, gentle wild things and you.

The one that I love so true is you!

Also dedicated to my darling children Ezra, Lilianna and Gabriel. May we all find hope and joy in this world.

ACKNOWLEDGEMENT

In the words of Robert Frost
"Two roads diverged in a wood, and I—
I took the one less traveled by,
And that has made all the difference."

Reflecting on St Paul's conversion and indeed my own and Jesus's teaching on The Way I would go further and even say:

"Two roads diverged in a wood, and I would have taken the broad way to destruction if it weren't for that blinding light. Instead I was compelled to follow the straight and narrow and He has made all the difference."

So my first acknowledgement is to God.

As a Christian project I also acknowledge the use of two Bible versions in both reference and influence over my writing, under a fair use policy:

Scripture quotations marked (ESV) are from The ESV® Bible (The Holy Bible, English Standard Version®), copyright © 2001 by Crossway, a

PREFACE

From the author:

It has been hard to decide what poems to include in this challenge and the resulting book. In the end I decided to put ones that promoted a certain set of ideals and beliefs.

This book has been titled A Holy Experiment. In 1681 - 1683 the famous Quaker William Penn founded the colony of Pennsylvania based on virtues that many still esteem today. If you don't know the story it is worth looking up. This was called The Holy Experiment. In many ways my poems reflect similar virtues and also come from a nonviolent ethic and Christian faith based view.

This little book is an experiment in writing and the propagation of deeply held values. Whilst I do not claim to be holy, nor that my writing is holy, hopefully it points in the direction of the only one who is truly holy. Jesus my king!

Day 1: QUESTIONS

Why are we here?
Why do the nations rage?
Why do the wicked prosper?
Where do wars come from?
Who am I Lord?
What must I do to be saved?
Revival, how long Lord?
In all our questions you have the answers.
Help us to keep asking questions.
Help us to listen.
Help us to be still and know that you are God.

*These lyrics have been developed into a song
which you can listen to on the authors blog.

Day 2: THE CHURCH IS NOT CLOSED

The church is not closed,
The church is deployed

Choose the fast
Loose the bonds

Free the oppressed
Break the yoke

Divide the bread
Feed the hungry

House the homeless
Clothe the naked

Darkness to light
Gloom to midday

Close your doors
Open your hearts

Church closed
Church deployed

Church deployed
Essential

Gospel Public services
Gospel voluntary services

Gospel homeless services
Gospel food banks

Graveside gospel
Bands of marriage gospel message

Live streams
Living streams

Gospel food pantry
Gospel soup kitchen

Gospel meals on wheels
Gospel grocery drop offs

Gospel food boxes
Gospel nappie provisions

Gospel clothes release
Gospel keyworker childcare

Gospel books
Gospel bibles

Keyworker vacancies
Witnesses sign up

His church will not disappear into the night
She will rise on the wings of the morning

Kingdom come
Kingdom coming

The church is not closed,
The church is deployed

* This poem was written during lockdown in the
covid-19 pandemic.

Day 3: KEEP WATCH

The watchman upon the wall.

Stand or fall?

Fiery darts aimed at all.

Keep watch dear friend,

Keep watch

The tongue a viper,

the wayward steps, stumbling,

lost,

thoughts frenzy,

tears fall,

lost, alone,

a war within and a war without.

Keep watch dear friend,

Keep watch

W.a.t.c.h

Words,

Actions,

Thoughts,

Companions,

Heart.

W.a.t.c.h

Keep watch dear friend,

Keep watch

The watchman upon the wall.

Stand or fall?

Fiery darts aimed at all.

O I stumble, o how I fall!

I can't do it alone my Lord

Keep watch dear God,

Keep watch of this heart of mine.

Day 4: WAR CHILD

Another body on an empty street.
No wave of flags for this child.
No red, white and blue.
No streets lined with mourners.
No drum beat or trumpet call.
No red flowers or wreaths.
No moment silence or vigil mass.
Worst of all: No faith, No hope, No love, None
is given.
This is the death of another nations child.

Day 5: FROM A SCREAM TO A WHISPER

There is a scream way down deep in my heart and soul.

A primitive scream of mourning, anger and pain.

A scream that should it erupt would shatter worlds.

A scream that if possible would awaken the ancestors and echo into the generations.

A scream that would make demons tremble and angels take notice.

It is not my scream alone, but a scream of collective force.

Fires and floods ravaged the years.

War and racial tension shook the earth.

Childish leaders oppressed the innocent and child like.

The species drained the earth of life and
resources.

Disease and pestilence attacked the species.

'A pale horse and the one who rides on it is death
and hell follows with him.'

What can hold back such a scream?

In my minds eye I see an empty old rugged
cross, an empty tomb, creation groaning in birth
pains, hope even in the darkness.

In my minds eye the scream becomes a whisper,
"Be still all peoples, be still creation, be still my
soul, be still and know that He is God."

Day 6: UPSIDE DOWN

On the road to Emmaus two fellows entered
fellowship with God.
'Did not our hearts burn within us...'
These fellows of the fellowship of the upper
room journeyed:
Sorrow? Fear? Is it over? Dead!
Joy? Courage? Just begun? Alive!
Turn the world upside down.
He turns hearts upside down.
The work is finished, but just begun.

Day 7: TESTIMONY

Grace Alone.

My heart yet afar off.

Christ dies for me.

My heart drawn to Him.

Christ rises for me.

Grace: Be still and know that I am God.

My heart broken.

Christ comforts me.

My heart angry at, the world, the flesh, the devil and even to my shame family and Him whom I have pierced.

Christ calms me.

Grace: Be still and know that I am God.

My heart yearning for a better world.

Christ encourages me.

Grace: Be still and know that I am God.

Lonely, My heart blessed with a beloved.

Desiring a child, My heart blessed with a baby.

My heart blessed with family.

Grace Alone: Be still and know that I am God.

***

The winds came.
God was not in that wind.
The earth shook.
God was not in that shaking.
The fire came.
God was not in that fire.
God was in the still small voice.

* Based on the authors Christian Testimony:

When I was young, my parents raised me in a
Christian home. The influence of the gospel lay
upon my life from a young age. I lived in the
Mission House owned by the Free Church. My

Dad worked as a local preacher and tour guide
and Mum was a caretaker of the Church building
next door as well as a Nurse and home help. The
Minister a Rev Macleod and his wife were so
kind to us and that has stayed with me over the
years. I wanted to give my life to Jesus after
hearing so many testimonies and seeing that
older believers I met at fellowships had
something or rather someone beautiful. I also
had a very deep conviction of my own sin and
need for a saviour. So the Lord drew my heart to
His and though young I invited Christ into my
heart and life. Though I have faltered and failed
many times along the way and the road hasn't
always been easy God had begun a good work in
me.

In my teens with a much fuller understanding
of the things of God I recommitted my life to
Jesus, or as one person put it I found assurance
of salvation. As a teen I took Free Church
communion for the first time, which is reserved
for those who are believers and who the elders
have examined as such and feel are ready. It was
a blessing.

In my later teens was a major denominational
split and a major family crisis. These things
impacted me. However, despite it shaking me

these things gave strength in the long run. I was inward looking until in a spiritual battle in my heart my eyes opened to the fact that others suffered still much more than I did.

When I went to University, I found that through my studying of Theology and Social Science that the troubles of human nature was not new, nor was the world's or my need for hope. In a rage one day I roared at God "Why do you allow such suffering in this world?" God seemed to have been saying "Why do you?" How could I ignore such a thing?

This idea of love was a spiritual awakening and the start of a profound stirring within my heart. I found my old path of blaming God for the world's woes was unsound. I discovered many woes are man made. Much further on in my story I could reflect in hindsight that God lives within the laws of cause and effect - laws he made, He lives by His own word and gives humans and angels free will. I could not blame God any longer.

Here are 5 other things I have discovered on my pilgrimage of faith:

1. Having for a time briefly looked at other faiths, by way of study, I concluded that though many faiths offer good ideas at times, Christianity in its truest form was the only faith I could find offering a much-needed saviour. Christian faith is not winning Brownie points with God, but is the person Jesus the Christ. It is less religion (man reaching God), more relationship (God reaching man in the person Jesus the Christ).

2. I could not save myself from sin or judgement, I needed and still need a redeemer. The heart of man's problem is the problem of man's heart. In this I was no exception. In the words of John Newton "I am a great sinner, but I have a great saviour."

3. Salvation is by Grace alone, through faith alone, in Christ alone for the glory of God alone.

4. This gift of salvation, does not remove the need for right living, but changes the motive. We must do good because it is right and because we love God and others, not to gain salvation or position with God. God is love, and whoever does not love is not of God. Good works do not save us, but Jesus saves us so we may do them. The early disciples were known for love to one

another and Jesus said his people will be known by their fruits.

5. It's important to be peacemakers, such are called the children of God. Christ came to reconcile man to God, and brothers to brothers. In a sense the phrase "not peace, but a sword", indicates division will come. In fact those who love the world, flesh and devil will hate Jesus' followers. But, those loyal to the saviour will "seek peace and pursue it" standing as lights in the darkness.

Some verses of note:

John 3:16 (KJV) For God so loved the world, that he gave his only begotten Son, that whosoever believeth in him should not perish, but have everlasting life.

Ephesians 2:8-10 (KJV) For by grace are ye saved through faith; and that not of yourselves: it is the gift of God: Not of works, lest any man should boast. For we are his workmanship, created in Christ Jesus unto good works, which God hath before ordained that we should walk in them.

2 Corinthians 4:6 (KJV) For God, who commanded the light to shine out of darkness, hath shined in our hearts, to give the light of the knowledge of the glory of God in the face of Jesus Christ.

Day 8: THE POOR MAN

We hid him. The poor man. His existence challenged our comfortable lives.
A prophet speaks out. The vipers take him out, on our wicked behalf. We say, "not in our name", but... How can the prophets compassionate humanity be tolerated when it challenges us this much?
Like trees with no fruit our true colours show. We store up. Moth and rust still win. The grass withers and the leaf fades.
A puff of smoke, a vapour. This to shall pass. The empires crumble and fall. Even the ecclesiastical tyrants meet their maker. The rich shall inherit the grave. Earth is for the others.

Day 9: SEE BEAUTY

He looks out the window and sighs.

A miserable day,
Grey sky,
Grey buildings,
Dirty old cars.

Sighs
Pauses
Looks
Lifts his pen.

***

In the midst of grey and dirt beauty!

Trees,
Leaves,
Pines,
Bushes,
Greens

Thriving in rain,
Finding nourishment.

***

So does his pen.

***

Purple,
Pink
Flowers.

Red,
Blue
Doors.

A weather beaten shed,
Vines,
Greenery.

Nature sometimes takes over where man has
been.

Yellow,
White
Fence.

Brightness,
Vibrance.

***

He looks hard
He sees beauty
He allows himself.

Day 10: GOOD FRIDAY

Scene 1 (The upper room): Take the bread. Take the cup. Be blessed. Foot washing. A final meal, a humble farewell.

Scene 2 (Betrayal): Watch with me! Bleeding tears. Anguish in prayer. Betrayed with a kiss.

Scene 3 (Peter and friends): Promises broken. Tearful regrets. Denial.

Scene 4 (The cross): A tear drop falls from the cross. A dying man's cry. The earth shakes. The temple trembles in the presence of God.

Scene 5 (Empty tomb): A king rises from the dark. The grave abandoned. Nature blooms in the presence of it's God. The victory accomplished!

Day 11: STOP

Remember to STOP sometimes STOP

"Be still and know that I am God. I will be exalted among the nations, I will be exalted in the earth!" *

Like the end of an old telegram message it felt as if God said STOP

Work study family Do do do STOP

Like the end of an old telegram message it felt as if God said STOP

Time and vaccines weaken the variants Debate debate debate STOP

Like the end of an old telegram message it felt as if God said STOP

Positively positive yet mildly mild symptoms STOP

Like the end of an old telegram message it felt as if God said STOP

Was it that or something else STOP

Like the end of an old telegram message it felt
as if God said STOP

Isolate quarantine pause reflect breathe Try to
breathe STOP

Like the end of an old telegram message it felt
as if God said STOP

Free and clear good to go STOP

Like the end of an old telegram message it felt
as if God said STOP

"Be still and know that I am God. I will be
exalted among the nations, I will be exalted in
the earth!"*

Remember to STOP sometimes STOP

* Psalm 46:10 ESV

Day 12: BEFORE THE BOMB

Before the Bomb:

Look down

Earth

Life

Light

The ball of blue

The home of hope

The garden is good.

After the Bomb:

Prophet purging

Slaughter of lambs

The ball of fire

The home of hell

'I am become death the destroyer of worlds.'

After the fire and into the light:

'We will become one with life the destroyer of
death.'

Swords to ploughs

Spears to pruning hooks

The garden to good

No turning back

Way

Truth

Life

Look up

* Originally written for a Scottish CND contest.

Day 13: DAY OF THE MARTYRS

Gathering of light.
Sacred assembly of love.
Age of war, hate, and strife.
The day of the martyrs has just begun.
Blood stained standing stones.
Anabaptists tears, angels song.
The day of the martyrs has just begun.
Ice cracks, foe falls.
Pilgrim saves.
To burning he must go.
Stands fast, dies slow, proclaims love for all to know.
The day of the martyrs has just begun.*

*Published in the anthology Poetic Velocity. This poem reflects on the powerful faith and love of many Christian martyrs. The main one is the story of Dirk Willems who was an Anabaptist Christian martyr. He was being hunted for his faith and he turned back to save his enemy when his enemy fell through some ice. Dirk was burnt at the stake for his faith despite his merciful gesture. He entered heaven with a clean conscience.

Day 14: READY FOR GOOD

The beauty of salvation

The Lord saves us

His own merciful grace

Ready for good

Saved

Excused

Ready

His handiwork

Re-created

Ready

In a world of

Dark

Hate

Oppression

Ready

Fruit

Blessings

The path

Ready

Opportunities

Service

Ready

Light

Love

Ready

Not saved by works

Saved by grace

Saved to do them

Ready for good

Are you ready?

Day 15: BEHOLD I MAKE ALL THINGS NEW

In the valleys of earth stood a tree.

A giver of good and evil, a provider of knowledge.

All kinds of seed giving plants covered the earth.

A beautiful forest.

In the gentle wind they sung hymns, a symphony of joy to the creator.

One day a darkness fell all across the earth.

It was a thick darkness.

The seeds shrivelled and died.

The trees fell one by one and began to rot.

Behold a dry barren wilderness.

No life, only death.

The prominent tree of the valley provides no
good fruit.

She is cut down and cast into the fire.

Hope seems lost.

A valley of dry bones and dead trees.

An unstoppable fire.

But, the gardener is at work claiming victory
over the fire.

The fire subsides, but he has only just begun.

His will is to breathe life into the earth.

Birds eat some of the seeds, rocks prevent
growth giving no roots, some choke in the
thorns.

But, in good soil the mustard seed falls.

From the smallest of seeds comes a lonely but
mighty tree.

Its roots dig deep and it spreads up and out.

The tree is planted by a river.

The river is a giver of life, the tree flourishes.

In the pale moonlight there is a shadow of a man
hung upon a tree.

The trees name is Life!

His blood waters the earth as does this midnight
storm.

The branches shake his outstretched arms.

Seeds fall like dead into the earth and from
thence they grow.

Though he dies yet he shall live.

Life! Beauty! Hope!

'Behold I make all things new.'

'Blessed are they that do his commandments,
that they may have the right to the tree of life...'
*

Behold I Make All Things New!

*Revelation 22:14 KJV

Day 16: TIME

'So teach us to number our days that we may get a heart of wisdom.' (Psalm 90:12 ESV)

Time goes marching on.

Many an empire has come and gone.

Yet we remain.

Watching the ticking clock and the sifting sands of time.

Time goes marching on.

Many a friend has been and gone.

Yet we remain.

Watching the ticking clock and the sifting sands of time.

Time goes marching on.

Many a soul has been lost and won.

Yet we remain.

Watching the ticking clock and the sifting sands of time.

Time goes marching on.

When our time comes, if we are remembered or not, will the love sown remain as time goes marching on?

Day 17: LOVE WINS

Love will win in the end, dear friends.
Love will win.
There are whispers of a word.
Amidst the chaos and confusion of a dark and
angry world, it echoes through the mist.
My heart heard this misunderstood little word.
It heard and was blessed.
The word love caused my heart to skip a beat
and my soul to become merry.
Could it be that even in mans darkest hours, love
still lives?
Indeed it lives and breaths all things pure.
But what is the meaning of such a word?
Could it be the joy of babes playing a merry
little din?
Is it the splendour of a spring morning?
Or the beauty of a maidens face basked in
sunlight?
Or perhaps its just a word we use in season to
gain something in return?
Maybe its just a word the poets like to write?
Nay, it is more.
Surely true love is self-sacrifice.
Its the laying down of ones life for a friend.
Even an enemy.

Its the will to bless those who curse us
To love our haters
To forgive our debtors as Jesus forgives his.
Love is not some superficial myth, but a dream
of things better.
It was love that allowed Gods own Son to give
himself into mans angry hands.
It was love that sent him beyond this realm to
prepare a peaceful place for us.
Our Promised Land, our Paradise.
Yes, behold, it is love that is the greatest thing!

*This poem won an award at allpoetry.com

Day 18: THE DIVINE KISS

For such a time as this,
The divine kiss.
God gives us position,
For the great commission.
His cause,
The greatest there ever was.
Unique character of our time,
Behold the shift in paradigm.
Clothe yourself in His apparel,
Neglect his voice at your peril.
No to cowardly sins,
Either way God wins!
For such a time as this,
The divine kiss.

*This poem won an award at allpoetry.com

Day 19: LEGIONS OF HOPE

We are the legions of hope.
We are his hands and feet.
We are the chosen.
Gifted by Grace,
Gifted to serve.
Called out of darkness,
Called to the light.
Voices in the wilderness,
His voice for the oppressed.
By His grace alone
We are the legions of hope.

*This poem won an award at allpoetry.com

Day 20: IT IS FINISHED

Finished
Bloody Palms
Bloody Crown
Bloody Ground
Bloody Nails
Radiant Light
Third Day Rising
Finished, but Just Begun

*This poem won an award at allpoetry.com

Day 21: THIS IS THE END

Lay down together, friends.
Roar lion, roar!
Silent lamb to slaughter.
A child will lead them.
Lay down together, friends.
Speak and nations bow.
Swords to ploughs.
The harvest is plenty.
Lay down together, friends.
Prince of peace.
Hallelujah, angels sing.
Saints awake.
Lay down together, friends.
Lay down on holy ground.
Lay down your weapons.
Lay down your burdens.
Lay down together, friends.
This is the end.

***

DONA NOBIS PACEM
GRANT US PEACE